Face To Face With A Saint

NEWER POEMS

JO DIRKS

First Produced in Australia in 2024
Reprinted with corrections 2024
by Spectrum Publications Pty Ltd
a: PO Box 75, Richmond, Vic. 3121
t: (+61) 1300 540 376
f: (+61) 1300 540 737
e: spectrum@spectrumpublications.com.au
www.spectrumpublications.com.au
on behalf Jo Dirks SSS

Copyright 2023 Fr Jo Dirks SSS
All rights reserved. No part of this publication may be reproduced in any manner without prior written permission of the publisher.

Cover Image of a young Dorothy Day used with permission from Marquette University
Cover Design: Rachel Price

ISBN 978-0-86786-123-5

Acknowledgements

I would like to acknowledge the unfailing support of Anthony Halliday in encouraging me to write these poems. He has gone further, by once again, setting some of the poems to music as he did with the earlier volume of my verse published as NEW POEMS 2021 by Spectrum Publications. This time he has written the music for six poems in FACE TO FACE WITH A SAINT. The songs are sung once again by the mezzo soprano Merlyn Quaife.

But this venture would not have been possible without the unstinting financial help of my two sisters, Rose Read and Trish Crisafulli. Lastly I thank my publisher, Peter Rohr, for bringing this project to completion. I acknowledge the friendly encouragement and support of Val Noone.

Sadly, my event organizer, Walter Remmen, died before this new collection of poems was ready. My condolences go to his widow, Brigitte, and her family. Finally I thank my superiors in the Blessed Sacrament Congregation.

CONTENTS

FACE TO FACE WITH A SAINT...1
SKETCH ARTIST.. 3
AUSTRALIA'S WUNDERKIND... 4
THE LANEWAY.. 6
THE JUMPING CASTLE 7
BALLOONS OVER MELBOURNE DAWN.. 14
ANNIVERSAR-ITIS 17
ST JALARTH... 18
DOWNSIZING.. 19
EVEN THE SUN MUST DIE... 20
THE BELLS OF ST GENEVIEVE... 21
RONALD MCDONALD... 22
BURNHAM BEECHES.. 23
THE WASTE LAND CENTENARY.. 25
THE NUN IN THE CAGE... 27
THE EIGHT MOUNTAINS TO BE CLIMBED.. 28
FR ED IS ONE HUNDRED.. 30
'OLD GIRL' SAYS MASS.. 31
ROYAL MINT HELLENIC MUSEUM.. 32
CUSTOMS HOUSE... 34
APPRECIATION LIMERICK... 35
JACK GINNIVAN.. 36
SLO-MO JO... 37
MARK II MAGPIES...38

MASSIVE DARK HOLE... 39

FRIENDLY GUIDE TO SCIENTIFIC ALPHABET.....................................40

MONT ST MICHEL.. 41

VINCENT VAN GOGH...42

SYDNEY OPERA HOUSE RE-OPENS... 43

HIGHER MATH GOSPEL...44

THE GREAT TEASE...45

TEN VIRGINS: AN UPDATE..46

HANDMADE UNIVERSE..47

ON HEARING THE DEATH OF QUEEN ELIZABETH II..........................48

LUMINESCENCE...50

WITHOUT A VISION..51

DREAMTIME...53

MY ROOM...54

RUNNING OF BULLS, SHEEP AND PENGUINS.....................................55

FERRY TO PORT ARLINGTON..56

SHARMA'S ARMY..57

SAUSAGE SIZZLE..58

KATYA ALEXANDROVSKAYA...59

BON MOTS FROM G. K. CHESTERTON..60

THE SUB-STATION...61

BURIED IN THE UKRAINE..62

BEGRABEN IN DER UKRAINE..63

THE LOST KING...64

FIVE ORDINATIONS.. 66

EARTHQUAKE	67
JAMES WEBB TELESCOPE	69
POEM TO MITCH AND JAKE	70
ONE WAY EMIGRATION	71
COUGAR ENCOUNTERS	72
THE ROAD TO ALBANY	74
THE LIGHT HORSE MONUMENT	76
PADRE WHITE LOOKOUT	77
FATHER BOB	79
BARRY HUMPHRIES	80
EUCHARISTIC WOMAN	81
NINGALOO	83
GABY UND HORST	85
TIGER TIGER	87
THE NEW BOY	90
CHILD OF HILDEGARD	92
ORIGINS	93
THE CHESS GAME	95
STRUGGLING WITH ARTIFICIAL INTELLIGENCE	96
OPPENHEIMER	97
THE VOICE OF GOD	100
THE MATILDAS	102
ETHICS OF THE SUMMIT	104
BEETHOVEN'S CHRISTOLOGY	106
ANDAMAN – NICHOBAR MISSION	108

SIGNS OF LIFE..110
THE DATE PALM...111
ANNUAL RETREAT 2023..112
CLIMATE CRISIS..113
HERE COMES THE SUN..114
SMACKY MAXY...116
HEARING CONFESSIONS 117
THE NEW GENERAL...119
SNOOPY, BART AND BLUEY 120
SEMINARIANS' DAY IN THE SIXTIES 121
THE WORLD WILL BE SAVED BY BEAUTY..123

FACE TO FACE WITH A SAINT
For Val Noone and lovers of Dorothy Day

Who gets to meet a saint in the flesh?
Not through a holy picture, statue, book, oil painting,
quote or internet. But to meet a real,
breathing, living, eating, feeling saint-to-be
that is a treasure beyond compare!
I did, as a baby priest, training wheels and all,
in August 1970 during my pastoral year,
at Harbord presbytery meeting up with Dorothy
and a small group of seasoned men,
not *episcopabiles*, nor the bêtes noires
exposed by Pope Francis, the career-seeking clergy,
but out of favour, 'left' and 'leftover' priests,
the Tony Newmans and Ted Kennedys.[1]
Roger Pryke and Jack Heffey laid the
ground-work when as seminarians they visited
the Catholic Worker farms and houses
in America coming home from Rome.
Dorothy, a grandmother with spirit,
her long silver hair plaited to her waist,

---

[1] *Dorothy Day in Australia* was published in Melbourne by Val Noone in 2020.

fired up not just against apartheid,
hunger striking, championing the poor.
No matter she had been a young communist,
lived out of wedlock, had an abortion even,
spent time in gaol, in May 2017 she became 'Venerable',
a saint desperately needed by the Church
in America, Europe and Australia.[2]
Now Pope Francis ranks her with
Abraham Lincoln and Martin Luther King!
Halleluia! Halleluia! Halleluia!

[26 March 2022]

---

[2] In May 2017, there was a formal presentation of the 'official' biography or Positio of the life of the Servant of God. It was accepted and approved, Dorothy Day was declared Venerable. Her granddaughter Kate Hennessy has already written an 'unofficial' biography in Dorothy Day: The World Will Be Saved by Beauty, Simon & Shuster, New York, 2017.

The following entry comes from the web-site of the Catholic Archdiocese of New York: 'The Archdiocese, which is sponsoring her cause, will gather the evidence and present it to the Vatican's Congregation for the Saints and Pope Francis. After carefully examining the information presented, the Congregation and Pope Francis will determine if she will be elevated from "Servant of God," to "Venerable," and become eligible for beatification and ultimately canonization.'
https://archny.org/news/dorothyday

SKETCH ARTIST

Hot north wind blew an unseasonal 30 degrees Celsius.
Near the three gawking skinny businessmen I spotted
the sketch artist in azure baseball cap and dark blue dress.
A small child sat for her as a proud mother watched.
I was next. As I sat down, I was told to relax and smile.
By-passers stopped and gazed as the pencils flew across
the paper, both old and young were grinning.
Trams and bikes whizzed past. I was twixt cathedral
spires and a Metro store, seeing nothing.
With a final flourish, signature and date, Emma asked
did I want a plastic cover? 'Yes' I said, not sure if I was looking
at myself or not. 'I'm from China' she said writing
'Melbourne City' on the A3 sheet, '23 September'.
It was me, on seeing the wart over my right eyebrow.
Paid with my equal third prize from the footy tipping.

[24 September 2017]

AUSTRALIA'S WUNDERKIND [3]

Tate bought and shown at twenty four[4];
trifecta at forty, Archibald, Wynn
and Sulman in 1978[5]; AO'd at fifty;
blazing comet streaking sky ultramarine blue
winking out at Lawrence's Thirroul,
booze and pills fed heart attack,
alone fifty three years young!
Your fluid curve of beauty, beach and bay;
angel graced akin a Mozart melody.
American Dream was not shown
in USA; *Alchemy twin*, 18 panels, one year
in creation was at the Kym Bonython;
you were there, strawberry blonde Afro.
Grünewald, Cimabue & Duccio fused into
the crucified Christ, your sculptor Jewish
friend Joel Elenberg bald with cancer;
your studio a shrine at Strawberry Hills

---

[3] The subject of this poem is Brett Whiteley.
[4] The Tate Modern Gallery is near Blackfriars Station, London, U. K.
[5] These three art prizes are awarded respectively, for the winner in the portrait, landscape and cultural category.

ever in the back lane arising Central.
Next time I visit, shall I take the light rail?

[8 September 2018]

THE LANEWAY

The laneway has not changed.
Once it was a pie-line served by the lay brothers
mid-afternoon for out-of-work or out-of-jail men, homeless, alcoholics;
they were served all alike when the monastery window
slid up and the frozen hands received
warm pies and tomato sauce.
Now moans, groans, shouts, ravings
float up from the laneway, drug fuelled
at all times especially night times but also mornings.
This morning the random groaning
was closer. I peeked out the window
and saw a bicycle ridden in crazy circles.
Each morning we chant common prayer
in the first floor oratory
greeting the Creator,
and praying to the Redeemer
for the lost souls in our midst.

[15 January 2022]

JUMPING CASTLE EVENT
1.

Castles don't jump. They are massive structures in stone;
think of the temple of Angkor Wat our near neighbour
rising like a mirage above the steamy jungle,
shimmering in the tropical heat,
ramparts dark against the light blue sky
housing hundreds of Buddhas in meditation.
Australia has its own castles in its creation story,
Bluff Knoll, Uluru, Purnululu, Warrumbungles' *Breadknife*,
Budawangs' Castle, Cradle Mountain, Barn Bluff and finally,
Blade or Federation Peak; shrines all, visited by their devotees.
Before Hillcrest we are mute, silenced and appalled
at the six young lives cut down before their prime,
consigned to the underworld where
they await their arisings
from the dead like
the Phoenix
of old.[6]

---

[6] Five students from Hillcrest Primary School in Devonport, Tasmania, died when a jumping castle went air borne with a gust of wind. Another student died after several days in hospital.

2.

These innocents were twelve years old; two were eleven,
all pre-puberty, children still and forever will be,
They have not heard the seductive call of the sirens
and satyrs nor experienced the turmoil of desire
as we their elders and mentors have;
they are forever young and ever will remain so.
Their purity, eagerness and freshness rebuke our weary sense
of déjà vu, cynicism and laissez faire.

3.

*In the land of Uz there lived a man
whose name was Job. This man was blameless and upright;
he feared God and shunned evil.
He had seven sons and three daughters* [7].
*when suddenly a mighty wind swept in from the desert
and struck the four corners of the house.
It collapsed on them
and they are dead*[8],
We could not understand what happened.
Six dead, three in hospital, a coroner's inquest pending;
Addison, Chace, Jalailah, Jye, Peter and Zane
all gone, all vanished, for all time,
remembered only by their smiles, joy and laughter,
buoyed by dreams & hopes for the future.
*"Naked I came from my mother's womb,
and naked I will depart.
The LORD gave and the LORD has taken away;
may the name of the LORD be praised".*[9]

---
[7] Job 1: 1 - 3
[8] Job 1: 19
[9] Job 1: 21

4.

Just as lammergeier vultures appear out of thin air when they are drawn
    to the place of death and lurk expectantly for the feast,
      or a chopper, blades thundering, will hover overhead,
        eager hands clutching tablets and pens poised
          to capture every detail that will emerge,
            they sit and wait like dingoes,
              to unearth Devonport,
              scavengers, skirmishing
            for the scraps and spoils
          of the imminent inquest.

5.

How do they cope: the sisters, brothers, parents,
grand-parents, aunts, uncles, cousins?
What sustains them in their anguish,
grieving, loss and longing?
What shared intimacy, what shared insight,
what shared wisdom strengthens?
The precious memories, the fond encounters,
the special moments comfort
yet pain in their uniqueness,
so fleeting and fragile,
like a puff of wind,
and is gone.

[14 March, 2023]

6.

Preparations
for the inquest are on hold,
says Coroner McTaggart, because
WorkSafe Tasmania won't release documents
deemed necessary for the hearings to be held
to determine what had happened,
and present the findings.[10]

[19 August, 2023]

---

[10] Media coverage of Tasmania.

7.

The findings:
'Jumping castle operator charged';
So screamed the headline on page eight
of '*The Australian*' on Saturday, 18 November
in 2023. It is alleged that Taz-Zorb failed
to comply with health and safety rules,
under Rule Two of the Health and Safety Act,
so says the Director of Public Prosecutions,
lodging a complaint in the Magistrates Court
in Devonport, for events on 16 December, 2021.
The company was then based at Launceston.
The matter is now before the courts.

[19 November, 2023]

BALLOONS AT DAWN
To Ignatius Vu SSS

After seven months of cancelled applications,
From mid-winter, spring and into summer,
Comes the message that the flight is on.
Perfect weather conditions are forecast.
I can't quite believe it, but make ready.
The alarm is set, I go early to bed
And wake up twice during the shortened night.
It's almost a relief when the nickering
Of the alarm starts up.
After washing I climb into the
Woollens even though the sun is full strength.
Iggy keys in *Amora* address to the GPS,
We exit the gate; no disruptions
As we glide into River St and park
In the basement and enter the lobby
Where there is a hive of activity,
Even at 5 am.
I ponder over the waiver questions:
'Am I under a doctor?', 'Have I had major heart surgery?';
There are three groups this morning.

Kit introduces Clem and we move outside to the van,
Which will take us to the launch site 6 km away,
a sports field by the Merri Creek,
Before that I make a joke, '*Shall we pick up Ed?*'
Iggy laughs. We arrive in the dark.
There are now five vans and trailers,
Disgorging people, giant baskets and acres of silk.
In the dark, the flames horizontal scything the black;
Gradually the silk starts to billow and rise aloft.
We clamber into the baskets and wait,
Mostly young couples and honeymooners.
Silently we soar upwards
The roar of the gas
Is all we hear.
The stillness surprises,
Tall red, azure, green, blue
And golden pears float
As each basket rotates,
And the horizon as well;
The vista goes west to Macedon,
North to Kinglake, east to the Dandenongs,
South to the Bay and the Tassie Spirit
Making for landfall at Station Pier.
The freeways are silvery ribbons,

FACE TO FACE WITH A SAINT

Eastern, Monash, Mornington.
The eye is drawn to the unusual shapes and sizes,
The city of Melbourne silhouette,
the unique Children's Hospital,
The dark green of the Fitzroy Gardens,
The shininess of the Tennis Centre,
The golf courses with their countless white sand traps,
Closer and closer come the multiple runways
Of Moorabbin airfield,
Our landing, soft and gentle.
The sun is now up, but we are down,
Buoyed up, walking still on air,
Despite the dewy grass.
In the morning traffic,
We are given our certificates.
Our smart phones
Receive proof
Of our ascent.
Now to a champagne,
Breakfast,
Praise God for 80 years.

[8 February 2022]

ANNIVERSAR-ITIS

Too many anniversaries! Stop, I want to get off,
but the wheels of time, great and small,
keep turning, the gears
are all engaged,
you have
60 years of religious profession,
the walking club has 70 years to celebrate
at Blackburn in the parish hall,
the fraternity was founded 80 years ago in 1942,
singing and dancing are being planned,
and now the ABC is spruiking its 90 years,
the Astronomy Society of Victoria has had its Centenary
already, marked with a special tour of the observatories
and telescopes at the Domain!
Can you have too much of a good thing?

[30 April 2022]

ST JALARTH
To Elisabeth Staberhofer

At the southern tip of the triangle of roads in Yarragon
stands the century old weatherboard church of St Jalarth,
serving the faithful and calling them to Sabbath prayers,
on the 1st, 3rd and 5th Sundays to the Holy Sacrifice.
Gladys Boonen left her estate for the renovation
of the church which is bright and filled with light,
with two a/c units near the ceiling, and O/H projector
and screen in place. Mass facing the people,
paschal candle, font and ambo all in place
Who is this saint? Born in 440 AD *Iarlaithe mac Loga*
was an Irish priest and scholar from Connacht,
venerated as the founder of the monastic School
of Tuam in 5th century Galway, when, as legend has it,
his chariot wheel broke, and the cross-wheel was born.
A live, breathing four footed canine, Samoyed-Labrador,
belonging to a Celtic parishioner beats every time
a fabulous heraldic griffin from a mythology tome.

[17 March, 2022]

DOWNSIZING

Downsizing is good, smaller footprint,
more compact, less shelves and cupboards,
fewer rooms, tiny gardens.
I visited a friend in a regional city,
parking outside in the street,
but greeted joyfully.
Took the scenic route round
the community rooms for meals and games
through the shrubby gardens
to the unit and invited to sit.
Cosy and comfortable were the easy chairs.
A small sewing table was nearby,
and a folding table could extra guests
or a computer and printer if you wish.
The kitchenette was the passage
to the bedroom and out into a small yard,
with pots and plants and a lock up shed
and friendly magpies.

[17 March 2022]

EVEN THE SUN MUST DIE

In a world of flux and change,
what remains?
When everything spins and whirls,
where is the centre?
When everything seems insane,
what makes for sanity?

[14 July 2010][11]

---

[11] The Eckhart Tolle workshops were among the most stimulating I conducted at RMIT

THE BELLS OF ST GENEVIEVE [12]

The Bells of St Genevieve are ringing.
Stop everything and listen to the sound;
Ding-a-ling, dong, ding-a-ling, dong;
Urgently, urgently, violin speaks to viol,
Again and again, calling the spirit, *Be Free*;
Calling all to the wedding banquet, inviting
Rich and poor, saint and sinner to the table
Viol speaks violin, harpsichord reinforces
Joyful summons, coming home to the centre,
All is forgiven, all is forgiven, come to the feast,
Heart bursting for joy, at home in God.

[19 March 2022]

---

[12] Composed by Marin Marais: Sonnerie de Sainte Geneviève du Mont de Paris.

RONALD MCDONALD
For Barbra Ady

'Ronald McDonald is dead', the phrase
repeated itself like a shrill cricket chirrup.
As it didn't seem real; it couldn't be so.
'He wasn't old enough to die!' Yet notice
in the newspaper was print real enough.
Eventually a funeral notice appeared.
'Jewish Kadisha will be held at Lyndhurst',
too soon, too far away to attend.
The Catholic farewell would be best,
next week at the Oakleigh parish church,
six priests present at least, Ron's mother,
a music teacher, was there; his brother,
read out his VCE class evaluation report
'Unshakeable' in belief at boarding school.
The schola sang J. S. Bach like angels.

[26 March 2022]

BURNHAM BEECHES
To Frank and Thea Arendse

The solemn stone pillars appear in the mist
on the right side of the Ferny Creek to Kallista Road,
the left being mainly Sherbrooke Forest.
I drive in to the unsealed narrow parking bay
and breathe in deeply the bracing mountain air.
I extricate my long legs from the car, put on
my Akubra, sally forth for the Burnham Beeches gate.
Wondering why this was a venture into the unknown,
family picnics at Ferny Creek, walks through Sherbrooke
Forest or many visits to the Arendse clan at Belgrave
might explain the omission. Past the story board
of Alfred Nicholas' rise in the pharmaceutical world,
thanks to his brother George cracking the chemistry
behind the humble asprin, ensuring his fortune.
You only get tantalizing glimpses of the grandeur
and the majesty of the multi-storeyed mansion,
peeping through the mountain ash, sassafras
and rhododendrons, once a home, private hotel,
then a children's hospital and a research facility.
Paths beckon downwards to the right, but I resist,

keeping to the access road leading into the creek, down to the lake and boat-house and tranquil pools limpid and placid, spanned by elegant bridgelets.

[28 April 2022]

THE WASTE LAND CENTENARY [13]
To Grant Fraser

We have had a century of discordant voices, offering
fragments of experience, joy, ecstacy and more,
promising the world, a broken world, sound bites,
offering little, '*THE BURIAL OF THE DEAD*',
reaches the Southern Cross sky; drug fuelled Tristan
with blonde Isolde in the Monash Medical Centre,
the fisher king looks on powerless in the picture frame.
'*A GAME OF CHESS*' came next, having its suspense
in the unknown endings of the contest; the neurotic sex
which defeats all gambits and cancels any outcome.
'*THE FIRE SERMON*' provides a counterpoint to all
that came beforehand in Augustine's plaint
of flame and Carthage extinguishment.
The snatch of the Aussie war poem about Mrs Porter
and her daughter is doggerel that has been enshrined.
'*DEATH BY WATER*', the Middle East trader
keeps the link to the Mediterranean Africa.
'*WHAT THE THUNDER SAID*' in the staccato[13]

---

[13] T. S. Eliot published THE WASTE LAND in the October 1922 edition of the magazine The Criterion.

reverberations of St John of the Cross, ramped up
into a Sanskrit alienating chorus of demagoguery,
the desperate longing for re-birth by water that comes
only from baptism. '*Set pools of silence in this thirsty land*'[14]
said the McAuley poem on Australian contemplatives,
but the orcs and trolls are winning, the dark lord
of Mordor is wasting every land of middle earth.

[30 April 2022]

---

[14] James McAuley, from A Letter to John Dryden, written on bluestone tablet at St. Patrick's Cath. Melbourne

NEWER POEMS

THE NUN IN THE CAGE
To All Asylum Seekers

The steel cage stands in front of the Park Hotel,
ironically opposite Abraham Lincoln Square,
shiny, unyielding, a prison for birds, not humans.
Inside the cage is an eighty seven year old woman,
Sister Brigid Arthur, advocate for the asylum seekers,
some of whom have been locked up for nine years
waiting for a decision which lets them walk free.
I started on this poem after watching Sister Brigid
at her work meeting former refugees on their farms,
firing up school students with her unique vision,
standing shoulder to shoulder with Tim Costello,
passionate about the human rights of these forgotten
people who have done nothing wrong, but made
to feel unwelcome where we are conscious
of the shortness of our citizenship as Australians.

[1 May 2022]

THE EIGHT MOUNTAINS OF ISRAEL
For the Dreamers and Hopers

Sister Joan Chittister has tasked the Catholic Church
in Australia with climbing eight mountains in Israel.
First is Mount Sinai, birth of the Ten Commandments;
some came away blessed by the goodness of God,
others with a stunted spirituality far from the Maker.
Mount Gilboa is next, the mountain of transition,
paving the way from Saul, grim defender of Israel
to David, psalmist and joyous dancer of the Lord.
Mount Olivet, where the passion of Jesus began
in the grove and the disciples were found wanting,
witnessed the young man fleeing naked into the night.
Mount Moriah, the mountain of questions not asked,
morality of abortion, role of women in the church,
third rite and what the bishops don't want discussed.
Carmel, the mountain of choice, keeping blind rules
or following the developing spirituality of communion.
Hermon, mount of transfiguration, where Jesus revealed
his self-giving death from which new life springs for us.
Gerizim, mount of recognition equality, the Samaritan
woman is accepted into the fold on her seventh attempt.

Beatitudes, mountains of bliss, where all hungers stilled,
holy and blessed, every summit and hollow is neutralised.

[2 May 2022]

FR ED IS ONE HUNDRED [15]

To Margaret and the Little Sisters of the Poor

Not the Queen, nor any of her substitutes,
ranging from her Governor, Prime Minister,
Lord Mayor on the one hand, neither to the
Pope or Archbishop on the other, whether
by telegram, signed letter or formal blessing
of the felicitations and congratulations, for Ed
there is one person whose approval counts,
only one approbation he is soliciting withal,
his sapiential Master and his sovereign Lord!
After Mass, I read out the dedication card
from Father Ignatius in Colombo, Sri Lanka
and presented special flowers to the centurion.
At the lunch on Sunday, tributes from his fellows
flowed and the *Happy Birthday* song sung again.

[15 May 2022]

---

[15] Fr Ed Wood SSS turned 100 on 15 May 2022.

'OLD GIRL' SAYS MASS

This is a strange conundrum. Here in my old school,
Our Lady of Mercy College, Heidelberg, to say Mass.
I remembered I had a photo inherited from my mother
Showing me in the centre of the first communion group
Among the boys, the girls were positioned behind us.
I captured this on my smart phone and the class teacher
Let each girl have a good look at the 1949 photograph.
Proof that a past pupil of OLMC was an ordained priest,
Verified at the college's jubilee when I attended
The banquet in Heidelberg Town Hall and laughed
At the comedienne's crudities and other one liners.

[13 May 2022]

ROYAL MINT HELLENIC MUSEUM

The staid Royal Mint transformed into a museum of Greek culture and history. There is an array of chambers; pottery, figurines, friezes from ruins, tombs commemorating the victors, then comes the hyperrealism of the sculptor Sam Jinks and his goddess Iris kneeling to scoop the waters of Lethe, almost human, but the soaring wings, ten feet high, negate such thoughts, pitch black and mysterious, despite her form as wholly naked common woman.

Displays of hoplites' helmets follow, encasing men in iron for combat, blocking sound, not sight Corinthian style best known; battering ram triremes, then come the glorious icons, a whole room of them, from St Aphrodite, Transfiguration, Pantocrator, Archangels Gabriel and Michael with his sword.

The fight for freedom from the Ottoman Turks is told in a video of battles and commanders galore. The Olympic Torches now appear, much later than the revival by Pierre de Coubertin. It was Carl Diem

proposing the torch relay run from Mt Olympus.[16]
Put on the VR[17] helmet and experience the temple
of Zeus, the chariots and their drivers, all sparkling
and shiningly new, are you, 'Ready! Set! and Go!'

[20 May, 2022]

---

[16] Carl Diem was a German sports administrator, and as Secretary General of the Organizing Committee of the Berlin Olympic Games, the chief organizer of the 1936 Olympic Summer Games.
[17] VR means 'virtual reality'.

CUSTOMS HOUSE

Here it stands, hemmed in on wall sides,
above all on the south side the railway
viaduct spoils the vista of the Bunjil
watching the Birrarang, the kangaroo
slaking its thirst at the water's edge.
Here too, the *Enterprize* had docked
on 30 August, 1835, a Sunday from
Devonport, the Lord's Day, so they
did nothing until Monday. The small tent
was replaced by a wooden hut which
leaked, then by a two-storey bluestone
house in 1841, a great public first for
Melbourne, but when gold was unearthed,
not grand enough, so the *Long Room*
was built, a huge imperial palace, that
impresses and silences the doubters,
we are in the fiscal and financial hands
of the Her Majesty's government Q. V.[18]

[20 May, 2022]

---

[18] Q. V. means Queen Victoria.

APPRECIATION LIMERICK[19]

There was an accountant by name of Mark
who ran fast marathons on the tanbark;
we wondered at his stamina and fitness,
for they helped his aptitude at business,
easy now, just a cakewalk in the ballpark.

[28 May, 2022]

---

[19] Presented to Mark O'Brien on his retirement at a staff farewell with many other good wishes.

JACK GINNIVAN

There was a bold young lad called J. Ginnivan,
Who came from the country round Castlemaine;
A cheeky forward with lots of blonde peroxide hair
With grass moves not in the book and knock out flair,
Doing each Saturday what only a Magpie larrikin can.
He changed into a hawk on lifting the premiership cup,
I judge his day at the races was the cause of the balls up.

[21 October, 2023]

SLO-MO JO

At the school play-ground Joe was quick
on his feet, the scabs on his knees proof
of derring-do or thoughtless foolishness
in equal measure. But now seventy years
later, here he is again in his worn runners,
track suit pants against the frost and cold,
not darting left and right, but shuffling
to reach the ball, grateful for short sets
and steaming tea mug in the club house.

[5 June, 2022]

VERSION II MAGPIES

The new Magpies have surprised the footballing world of the AFL, abandoning their previous play-book, attacking through the corridor, the short way home, whenever they can, a chaos game plan, and guess what, it's working! Demons, Hawks, Dockers, Saints – all despatched in the past month
Even though their best ruckman won't be back for a month,
the full back has retired from injuries, the team includes
four untried sons of former proven club champions,
an explosive midfielder out of gaol on bail,
an ageing captain with basketball skills
and an American seven footer who
plays with glasses, else blind,
and a brand new coach
also again learning
but doing well;
muscling
into the
eight.

[15 June, 2022]

MASSIVE DARK HOLE

Wanna feel puny? Try this! '*The black hole swallows an Earth equivalent every second, and is seven thousand times brighter than our Milky Way Galaxy,*' with the right gear is seeable from your very own backyard. This discovery has been made by an international team of scientists led by astronomers from A.N.U., in Canberra. The whole story to all this is but nine billion years by which time the hole has grown quite large indeed: '*It is five hundred times bigger than the black hole in our own Galaxy*', said researcher Sam Lai.

[16 June, 2022]

FRIENDLY GUIDE TO SCIENTIFIC ALPHABET
To Shane Dooley

C means a hundred;
C° to F°: Celsius to Fahrenheit Conversion Formula
To convert temperatures in degrees Celsius to Fahrenheit, multiply by 9/5 & add 32;
$E = mc^2$, Einstein's famous equation, energy = mass x speed of light;
= means equality;
$F = ma$ which is Newton's law, Force = mass x acceleration;
G stands for a billion;
K means a thousand;
L means fifty;
M means a million;
% means Percent, 1% = 1/100;
Π is a symbol in maths for circle formulas, specifically 22 over 7;
√ is the square root symbol, so $\sqrt{9} = 3$;
SUPERSCRIPT⁴ means the number is raised to the power of 4, $2^4 = 16$;
T means terabyte, so 1 TB = one million terabytes, one thousand GB;

[16 June, 2022]

MONT ST MICHEL

There it stands on the horizon, a tiny silhouette,
a smudge, but one a thousand years old,
for the English, wanting to capture the mount,
for the tourists, who come to photograph the hill,
for me, hunting for the essence of the place.
The mirage solidifies itself on my approach,
walls, towers, battlements and the path always
going up. The chapel of the patron, St Michael, stands
on the summit where the daily round is praise,
worship and giving back to God his divine gifts.

[19 July, 2022]

VINCENT VAN GOGH

You were the artist who could not sell
your paintings in your life-time, now
through the quirks of the art market,
they are among the most expensive.
Fuelled by the quarrel with Gauguin,
fellow outsider, was it a rehearsal or
did you really shoot yourself?
A pastor's son, yourself a pastor, had
a horror of suicide, a cutting off short
God's creative work. The shot was to
the abdomen. Unlikely target for ending
your life. There are suspects, two youths,
who taunted you. There is a weapon,
a pistol discovered in an Auvers field.
Motive – yes, you talked about it a lot,
but did not do it. Your hosts discovered
you alive at 9 pm out in the fields. Theo
rushes from Paris to be with his brother.

[21 July, 2022]

NEWER POEMS

SYDNEY OPERA HOUSE RE-OPENS

What music do you chose to re-open the Opera House?
Not an easy one! Last century it might have been after
we all attended church, but not now, when the arts are
called to heavy lifting with all things that are ecstatic.
Mahler's Symphony No. 2, is a suitable heavyweight;
Klopstock's ode, '*The Resurrection*', we come home.
A Sturm und Drang genre beloved by the Romantics,
who believed human spirit was invincible, until the
unknown iceberg taught the builders of the *Titanic*
sinking, the missing life boats resulting in tragedy.
Simone Young took all this in her stride, switching
from the Hamburg State to the Sydney Symphony:
Relentlessly, Mahler builds his massive forces into
an accumulative blaze of rapturous affirmation:
voices rise in ecstasy, bells chime, the augmented brass
choir swells, and a vision of eternal life unfolds before
our eyes, if but for a few moments of glowing certainty.[20]

[23 July, 2022]

---

[20] Edward Seckerson, Program Notes, Sydney Opera House, 21 July 2022, p. 19.

HIGHER MATH GOSPEL

M2L or Lm2, being the title of the new feast
on the 29th of July, Martha, Mary and Lazarus.
Spirit's algebra trumping the world's arithmetic
yet again; it was ever so, Hannaniah losing to
Jeremiah the prophet; the priest Amaziah wrestling
with Amos; king Ahab contesting with Elijah;
Naaman the leper proudly arguing with Elisha;
Jesus before the high priest Caiaphas; apostles
Peter and John before the Jewish Sanhedrin;
brilliant deacon Stephen resisting Saul of Tarsus
Henry VIII 'legally' killing his queen-spouses,
Melissa Jaffer plays a crone in film *Fury Road*
averse to patriarchy[21]; Lidia Thorpe sworn in as
Greens senator in Canberra; and today we have
Fr Frank Brennan, called *'a meddlesome priest'*
by Paul Keating, engaged for our September
day of reflection, conversion and discussion.

[2 August, 2022]

---

[21] Melissa Jaffer is an Australian actress who portrayed the Keeper of the Seeds in the George Miller directed film *Mad Max: Fury Road*.

THE GREAT TEASE

It is the biggest unanswered question
in the universe, 'Are we alone?' Our
mathematicians tell us that there is no
limit to the number of life forms out there.
But we do not have one confirmed datum
of evidence, not one shred to say otherwise.
Until we do have some proof, we repeat
our circle dance round the stars and suns.

[3 August 2022]

TEN VIRGINS: PARABLE UPDATE

A newer version of the parable is available for download.
Ten virgins are invited to be bridesmaids at a rural wedding,
Five had brought their power packs for their smart phones.
Five did not have any back up. The bridegroom was late.
At midnight the cry was heard, 'The bridegroom is coming'.
The bridesmaids all flicked on their smart phones.
The wise ones switched over to their power packs.
The foolish ones found their charge had weakened,
Their displays were winking out. "What shall we do?'
They wailed.

[26 August 2022]

HANDMADE UNIVERSE

Approaching the dark gray pillars of the State
Library, the fluttering colourful banners evoked
creativity, women and a dark blue map of the stars.
For an inveterate map-lover this was tantalizing
in the extreme, to say the least, as I entered
the lobby and asked the attendant where was
the 'Handmade Universe' exhibition ?
Emboldened by his reply, 'take the lift and
turn left', I quickly passed the art gallery,
paused before the Lebanese alchemy artwork
and entered a long gallery where stars glowed,
mesmerizing, beckoned. There on the right side,
a knitting machine stood, just like my mother's,
save she had a fear of all computers, and this
one had mapped eighty eight constellations
of the universe which lit up star pathways
in colours when you activated the notebook
nearby. Right in front was the wondrous feat
of seven extended knits seamlessly joined,
dark blue field angled before the viewer, azure.

[1 October, 2022]

ON HEARING THE DEATH OF ELIZABETH II
To John Pugh SSS

Early in the morning came the sad news on the radio, that the Queen had died. Most of my life she had been the monarch. I was a pre pubescent schoolboy in short pants in Grattan Street on the fringe of 'The Shop', equal to 'The Firm', I suppose, as she passed. A few years later Mother and I took the oath of allegiance and we became Australian citizens in a ceremony at Brighton Town Hall. Our Liberal Prime Minister promised the U.S. our help, in their crusade against Communism. That meant I could be called up via the ballot to fight in the Viet Nam jungles. None of this happened, for I joined the SSS and many years of studies followed. Brother Joseph felt that the Queen was worthy of being sainted, certainly Pope Francis praised her unstinting service and faith. She was fond of Basil Hume, *'My Cardinal'*, she said. No trumpet fanfare for Diana; that is already ancient history, but her tall sons live on, heartbeats from the Windsor throne, making their way, William and Harry. The tributes flow. The 24 hour notice of a service at St Paul's Cathedral is too short an interval. Queen Elizabeth deserves better. We wish to praise her

in our public voice, song and music. Are we really ready
for King Charles III and his consort Camilla? Albanese
selects ten Australians to accompany him to the funeral.
ELIZABETH REGINA II OBIT - 8 – September - 2022.
After England's pomp, the ceremony at Parliament House
Canberra showed our human side, indigenous and wattled.

[21 September, 2022]

LUMINESCENCE

'And God said, "*Let there be light*,"
and there was light. And God saw
that the light was good. And God
separated the light from the dark.'
Matter, worms, beetles know how
to produce lumes of light to attract,
repel, deceive a mate, predator or prey.
Squid know the power too, the crabs
don't. Dolphins do too. Mammals
are in awe, even the nocturnal ones.
Oceans can glow and glitter like stars
in the sky due to bio-luminescence,
a natural process allowing microcells
to make light in their organisms.
Dolphins lucked into the plankton
rich waters; bio-lume did the rest.
David Attenborough not needed.

[23 September, 2022]

WITHOUT A VISION
To Melissa Jaffer

… the people will perish', said the prophet long ago.
Rev Alan Walker, head of Wesley Central Mission,
made this the slogan of his campaign to capture
the youth of Sydney for Christ. He organised a
a country fair for Christ at Arcadia, renaming it
Vision Valley, and to keep the new disciples in tow
he invited them to Daniel's Den in his basement
dungeon in Pitt Street. The time has come to raise
trumpets to our lips and sound the battle cry once more.
Kevin Ouvrier knew the challenge for his small band,
he had the vision, but lacked the know-how, technique,
savoir-faire to bring it to gob-smacking reality. Sarah
Gilbert is on about the same pursuit in her draft story
of the Sister Servants' journey from Armadale enclosure
to the 'shambolic' Redfern liturgies with Father Ted.
Time for telling your story, and being listened to with
compassionate hearts, so you could unburden yourself,
and leave your problem at the table, returning to life,
lighter, unfettered, free. Betty gone, Maureen gone,
Vianney gone, now you Marian, Marie and Melissa,

are the keepers of this dream, you have each tasted Christ in this quest of mission, not ministry, to grasp the essence of Christ risen, a body unembraceable, but real, spiritual, transformed, in the poor, the black and the marginalised that are all around us waiting.

[30 September, 2022]

DREAMTIME

Gerry Kearney encouraged us to dream afresh.
We marvelled at her connexions with Myanmar,
Staunch Bhuddist mother and Catholic father,
And her love of First People on remote Kiribas,
And later at Mackay; when she felt the icy blast of
Government report that said 'Not administrative
Enough'; Sonia Wagner said, 'I would have worried
If not pastoral enough.' A tuck shop fail. Swamped
With warmth and love; Jason Donovan and chorus
Of kids with songs to show us the way and Ant.
Adjusting the audio to its proper pitch and volume.
Secret Garden is singing of joys shared and treasured.
I said I have poems inside me waiting to come out.

[4 October, 2022]

MY ROOM

A whining noise comes from the dark street below. Work has resumed on the sewer upgrade promised by the city council, not as disruptive as the drilling, jack-hammering and grinding of last week; sounds lower and slower in decibels, then stop. Oh, bliss of silence, for how long? The icon of *Christus Pantocrator* gazes serenely from its central location. Outside leaves of the avocado tree filling the windows to left and right. A greyish bird thudding into the clear glass, dashing itself again and again, with blind force seeking a way to come inside, desperately repeating this manoeuvre. The whining has resumed. I will close the glazed glass window tonight and double down on the divine presence. I am at peace on the recliner, gift of a deceased confrere.

[16 October, 2022]

RUNNING OF BULLS, SHEEP AND PENGUINS

Pamplona has the annual July *Running of the Bulls*, on the feast of Saint Fermin, each runner is decked in white with a red kerchief around the neck, down its narrow cobblestone lanes made famous by the author Ernest Hemingway in love with his Spain. Mont Saint Michel has the daily black face sheep run, when the flocks leave the salty grass pasture of the lush grazing opposite the historic mount, waiting to charge across the road, forking off left and right to their homes, corrals and pens. Philip Island also has a daily parade, the fairy penguins, food heavy, assemble on the beach each night, waiting for one another, peeling off with precise awareness to home burrows where their hungry young chicks await them.

[20 October, 2022]

FERRY TO PORT ARLINGTON
To Mark and Marie O'Brien

All trams headed west on the Hoddle grid disgorge their human cargo in Docklands at the esplanade where *The Bellarine Flyer* awaits them, double storied above, twin hulled below, a sleek white catamaran craft. Prior departure, '*Happy Birthday*' is sung as the featured guest boards. We reverse, rotate and glide from the jetty, brig *Alma Doppel* on the left, under the *Bolte Bridge*, on the right the massive *Amity City* from Nassau and the container docks with their giant cranes, now past the tiny punt taking cyclists across the Yarra, then past the Svitzer tugs, the *Daintree*, *Eureka*, *Marysville* and *Otway*, under the West Gate, past the dredge Wallenius *Nabucco* to open waters at Williamstown, where the throttle is opened to the max. We follow the channel, freighters to port, yachts and pleasure boats to starboard. Sea is flat like a mill-pond. Not a white cap to be seen. I know I'm no sailor, so am grateful. The rowdy crowd on board repeat their boozy birthday song as our destination nears. We find the marina entrance, pull up at our wharf. Mark's friendly face greets me.

[17 November, 2022]

SHARMA'S ARMY
Colin & Susan Fowler

Invitations went out on time. Now the day
has come. Set up successful. Food prepared.
Everything is ready, laid out, neat and tidy.
Where are the guests? Some jokes are made.
'Go to the streets and by-ways, invite anyone
who is ready'. Ant. arrives. The meal is blest.
Dora, Suzanne, Loretta and Noreen, loyalists
all. Mike and Robbie welcomed, father and son
Philip and Tessie arrive. Teresa helps serve.
Little gifts are handed out by Sharma. 'I may
not do this much longer', she tells her band of
volunteers, 'I am thinking of retirement'. Covid
has been a nightmare for her, even this morning
she got many cancellations and apologies at the
last minute. That is pretty tough. God bless her.

[2 December, 2022]

SAUSAGE SIZZLE

Fifteen kilograms of pork and beef snags
A most generous gift which transformed
By the apostle students into common fare
Duplicating the multiplication at Tabgha
The loaves and fishes that fed the hunger
Courtesy of the electric fryers to barbecue
The humble sausages, eagerly devoured
By the Sunday evening worshippers who
Have their gastric juices activated by the
diligence, work and friendliness on show
Now have struck gold.

[4 December, 2022]

KATYA ALEXANDROVSKAYA

Katya, the fairy tale of the ice gliding dance princess,
melded in a foreign union of north and south, female
and male, wondrous to behold, picture perfect pairing,
matched ambitions yielded instant success. The price
was high, way too high, but wins silenced the dangers
and you risked all, especially your own birth right self
in a new land and country, a newly minted nationality
where you had nothing, language, customs, festivals,
without support of your mother, father being dead,
a pressure cooker world, unsustainable, not in bursts
even; to the Moscow twilight you returned, trying to
salvage something from shipwreck of a dance career
frozen by epileptic seizures on the ice you had owned,
little empress of ice dancing, why did you want to be
the best? I grieve, I lament your death at twenty years.

[13 December, 2022]

BON MOTS FROM G. K.
To Edward Wood SSS

'*Let good things run wild*', said Chesterton.
That is pretty good! What else did he say?
'*that thanks are the highest form of thought,
that gratitude is happiness doubled by wonder.*'

'*Poets have been mysteriously silent on the
subject of cheese*'. But now they asking how
can you tell a stinker from a cheddar. Easy,
one breath through the nostrils, oh the smell.

'*Praise should be the permanent pulsation of the soul.*'
This would put the clinics & GPs out of business
and put the NATIONAL HEALTH SERVICE
into black, which has never happened before.

'*If there were no God, there would be no atheists.*'
Ah, very true, but would we be so heartless though?

[18 December, 2022]

THE SUB-STATION

The electric sub-station stands inside the Fitzroy Gardens
No tin shed, but solid brick, well planned, with a tiled roof
Overhang on all sides, with friendly seats underneath, tailor
Made for Melbourne's unpredictable weather, but now caged,
Locked off by a wall steel barricade. The winos in the SEC fifties
Never had to face this kind of unwelcome. The proud plaques
Testify to '*Citipower*', fourteen of them, cemented in the brick.
The station has survived where my old school did not, save
For one bluestone Georgian tower. The one solitary padlock
Traps the morning light. No empty threepenny dark bottles
To collect and re-cycle for the smelting nouveau glass factory.

[26 December, 2022]

BURIED IN THE UKRAINE
To Horst and Gaby Dallwitz

He lies buried in Ukrainian earth
A long way from the country of his birth,
The son of a lemonade brewer which was enough
To have him classed a kulak and then smeared
In the famine ordered by Stalin who wanted
To purify the Soviet Union of the farmers.
You had carried a photo of your Hilde and
your new born son, all three pierced by a bullet,
You falling to the ground on 14 June, 1942
In Balaklava on the Crimean peninsula.
As you entered into eternity, inexperienced
And unfulfilled architect, the new world
Greeted you for, heroes are not unsung,
Thanks to Putin and his special operation,
O my long lost, loved and dearest father.

[15 May, 2023]

NEWER POEMS

BEGRABEN IN DER UKRAINE
Zu Horst und Gaby Dallwitz

Er liegt in der Erde in der Ukraine
weit weg vom Vaterland, ein Kind
eines Limonadebräuer, das war genug
als einen Kulak angedeutet zu sein, und
dann verschmierten in den Hungersnot
von Stalin, der möchte die Bauern raus
die Sowjetischen Union reinigen lassen.
Du hast ein Foto deiner Hilde und Sohn
versteckt über deinen Herz bis ein Schuss
alle Drei durchbohrte und Du zum Boden
tot gefallen bist, am 14 Juni 1942 im Krim
in Balaclava. Als Du in Ewigkeit eingetreten
bist, O unerfahren und unerfüllter Architekt,
hat dich die neue Welt begrüsst, die Helden
nicht ungemein sind, dankbar Herr Putin
und sein Sonderwirkung, O mein lang
verlorenen, geliebten vermissten Vater.

[1 Januar, 2023]

THE LOST KING

Richard III was our text for Intermediate English.
Much maligned, a villain who killed the princes
In the Tower, following in Herod's footsteps,
So we thought, such was Shakespeare's talent,
Converting a new widow into prospective bride
Within a scene on a stage, razzle-dazzle indeed.
Propaganda was invented and used long ago,
Why do we always think we were the first
To use psychology for our own ends?
Neither a hunchback, nor a murderer
The real King Richard battled his foes
In a field, now an urban car parking lot,
The former Catholic Greyfriars church.
The skeleton exhumed showed a blow
To the skull; the spine was curved,
Confirming it really was Richard.
Later DNA testing confirmed
The identification of the remains.
Amateur historian Philippa Langley
Was awarded an MBE from the Queen

And Richard was given a royal burial
On 26 March 2015 in Leicester Cathedral.

[31 December, 2022]

FIVE ORDINATIONS

Five newly ordained men at one blush,
five blessings, living gifts of the Spirit
is impressive for most religious orders!
The Salesians asked us if they could use
our Church. None of their churches was big
enough. Tim Costelloe was ordaining prelate,
four hours away from his dry, native Perth
assisted by Tony Ireland, one time Master
of Corpus Christi Seminary. Ben Ho graciously
said yes, offering Johnny and Pete as Acolytes.
Could this be the future? Some form of sharing,
partnership even, as the Archdiocese had said
no, though we had not even asked the question.
Speculation only, but its tantalizing to ponder
the possibilities and outcomes for the future.

[28 January, 2023]

EARTHQUAKE

How dare I write about the earthquake
in Turkey and Syria! Especially in Syria,
where the people have suffered so much
from human conflict and war. Nature has
stepped in and flexed its muscles, shown
us the naked anguish of Job once again,
grieving fathers cradling dead children
in their arms or dead mother, umbilical
still attached to the living child rescued
from the chaos and debris of collapsed
apartments. What of lucky survivors?
Are they really fortunate to have lived,
their loved ones have perished, wives,
sons, daughters, fathers, mothers, all
have gone into everlasting darkness,
whilst they endure freezing weather,
the bitter cold in the icy wilderness,
where the frost clamps with brutal
strength fragile, fearful buds of love,
and hopes and dreams of a morning

better than the chaos of what is left,
cold refrigeration of pain memories.

[9 February, 2023

JAMES WEBB SPACE TELESCOPE
To Tony Lawless

The JWST is an extraordinary piece of AI[22],
It's praises are sung in the media, its photos
of deep space truly amazing, awe inspiring,
but when all is said and done, it is a bit of AI,
no more or less. Maybe I am an ungrateful
beholder of a wonder of our times and age.
I still await answers, what is dark matter,
what are black holes? Teilhard de Chardin's
noosphere is very much with us, but it is
not the last word. Jesus spoke to Moses
and Elijah on the mount. The voice said
'This is my son in whom I am well pleased.'
When the theremin[23] begins its hypnotic tone
with its eerie, unearthly etherphone noise
no matter who generates or produces it,
and all fall silent in shocked amazement, I
will not genuflect or bow down on my knees
to the golden dish hurtling through space.

[25 February, 2023]

---

[22] Artificial Intelligence.
[23] Named after Leon Theremin who invented the musical synthesizer, popularised by the theme for Dr Who.

POEM TO MITCH AND JAKE
For Mitch and Jake Crisafulli

You need to be much thanked for giving me
Your special room at Nana's and Grandpa's.
You are not my Sons, but Grand Nephews.
You remind me of the great English bard,
Born in Africa, author of '*The Hobbit*',
John Tolkien, who wrote it for his boys,
Each evening story time. You, Mitch have
a magic island yklept, Skellig Michael,
Where the filming of the Jedhi took place.
And you, Jake, named after the French variant
Of James the Great entombed in Spain, source
Of a cris cross of pilgrim paths. May you be
Both blessed with wit, play and questing,
all the days of your lives until the sun sets.

[1 March, 2023]

ONE WAY EMIGRATION

It is a fact that the migration rush
out of Russia is much the same
as once it was to escape and leave
the iron curtain out of the Soviet
Union. The scalps of Klaus Fuchs,
Kim Philby, Guy Burgess, Donald
Maclean, Sir Anthony Blunt, not
withstanding, these defectors were
outnumbered by those desperate
hordes that burrowed, tunnelled,
flew, bribed and escaped into the
welcoming freedom of the West,
and the waiting arms of democracy.

[3 March, 2023]

COUGAR ENCOUNTERS

On Saturday mornings the papers are filled with exotic tales of strange beasts that are seen in the bush, big cats, panthers and cougars. The cougars have become the favourites by far, for stories abound of U. S. warships docking at Fremantle in the forties. Four cougar kittens too big to handle, were released by the sailors, one pair in the bush at Fremantle, another pair at Bunbury. Then came the circus stories. The only one involving cougars escaping into the wild was an overturned trailer, but as always, documentation was lacking. Another was the Great Moscow Circus, which did have cougars. Another sighting was on the old road to Jurien Bay of a beast like a panther with a long tail, was it the legendary "Nannup Tiger" on a prowl? The thylacine was supposed to be extinct, but the sightings go on and on. However cougars will always trump dogs and foxes, or eagles and cats, and the poor thylacine.

[4 March, 2023]

THE ROAD TO ALBANY

Early departure from Mindarie meant
full peak hour traffic on the Mitchell
Freeway and road works, adding a lane,
excavators, tip trucks, the chief offenders.
Things improved after the Perth exits,
new skyscrapers at Applecross , where
I first played social tennis. We took the
Armadale exit and continued south.
We picked up new strangers, B doubles,
even triples, and we're grateful for the
frequent overtaking lane that enabled
us to safely pass these monsters. We
stopped at *The Woolshed* in Williams.
Glorious blueberry muffins stilled our
hungers and lattes quenched our thirst.
The merino pullovers were reduced by
fifty seven dollars to one four two $ $.
A shield proclaimed we were in the shire
of Plantagenet. And at Mt Barker came
'*The Stirlings*', of happy memories.

We pressed on, stopping twice at red
traffic lights as half the Albany Highway
was closed for safety improvements.
We coasted into Albany looking for a
whale outside our motel. The whale had
relocated up the hill behind our rooms.
We made a beeline for the brig *Amity*,
outside the Great Southern Museum.

[9 March, 2023]

THE LIGHT HORSE MONUMENT[23]

Atop Mount Clarence is the bronze statue
by Bertram Mackennal of two horses, noble
under fire and two soldiers; an Aussie is
sheltering a Kiwi whose horse has fallen
in conflict. This tribute was destroyed
by a mob during the Suez riots of 1956.
Menzies ordered the shards brought
back to Australia, where the statue was
faithfully remade in a Sydney studio.
From Convoy Lookout you see the harbour
laid out before you, the thirty six ships
of the first convoy, plus ten Kiwi ships
and two months later, the fourteen ships,
three Kiwis and AE2 of the second convoy
that sailed afterwards. All 21,500 Aussies,
8,500 Kiwis and the gallant 12,000 horses
from both countries were on their way to war,
not to Flanders as expected, but the Middle
East. One horse returned to New Zealand.

[10 March, 2023]

---

[24] There are several monuments dedicated to the Light Horse Brigade around Australia. This one is at Albany at Mount Clarence in W. A. and celebrates the military alliance with New Zealand.

PADRE WHITE LOOKOUT

Arthur White, born in the U. K., ordained
priest, suffered from an ear infection and
migrated for health reasons coming from
Williams to see the convoy being readied.
He enlisted in 1916 as an AIF Chaplain with
the ANZAC troops. Dubbed '*The Padre*',
he returned to Australia and led a dawn
service at Mount Clarence, in 1930, as
the vicar of Albany, which caught on,
so that now the dawn service is the
traditional way the fallen are recalled.
A disabled walkway from the Light
Horse Memorial to the summit rock
is flanked by stainless steel handrails
and metal mesh flooring. As emeritus
rector of St John's, he said, '*guard
closely that wonderful Dawn Service
and the other ceremony that had developed
from it, particularly the laying of the wreath*

in the waters of the Sound[25]. He died in 1954 aged 71, just retired at Herberton, Queensland.

[12 March, 2023]

---

[25] The reference is to King George Sound, the ocean waters next to Princess Royal Harbour, Albany.

FATHER BOB

Dad knew how to pick a maverick,
the one that doesn't fit in, that stands
out from the crowd, that amuses, enter-
tains, challenges our ways of thinking.
Father Bob was one such, knocking
with glee on the coffin at a parish funeral.
He had a difficult start to life, with a
violent alcoholic father and he youngest.
He spoke up for Mother Church, not
father church, forming '*Open Family*'.
He had run ins with Archbishops Pell and
Hart, and it cost him dearly, having
to retire at 77 and then start up his
'*Foundation*'. Nothing but praise after
death. Ex-premier Jeff and Comrade
Dan sang his praises, and has offered
a state funeral. What would Bob have
quipped? '*If you limit your contribution
to the world to praying, you are no
earthly use to anybody*', so said
the larrikin, curmudgeon-priest.

[22 April, 2023]

BARRY HUMPHRIES

The Mark Knight cartoon said it best. Barry Humphries arrives before a frazzled St Peter at the pearly gates of heaven, accompanied by over polite Dame Edna Everage and boozy Sir Les Patterson. One of the founders of the Melbourne International Comedy Festival, Baz was barred coz of his comments about trans gender performers. Sarcasm and satire are always naughty, and out of control.

[24 April, 2023]

EUCHARISTIC WOMAN
*To Johnny Nguyen Van Cho
and Pete Nguyen*

1.
Woman, great is your care and love,
first at Cana, you did show full faith,
when groom and bride ran out of wine;
the steward's wonder at unasked gift.

2.
Show us your love, we cry to you;
we seek the meaning of his cross
show us your Son, not count the cost,
in solidarity and prayer.

3.
Show us your Child, we cry to you;
we would his disciples be,
show us your Prince, that we might live
Spirit filled as God's children.

4.

Show us your Son, arisen;
We are his kin, by your Fiat.
Help our poor faith, we trust in you,
True disciples, all thanks to you.

5.

Maid, great is your faith and love,
Your womb that bore, your bosom
That suckled the hungers of the child
That all creation cannot compass.

6.

Woman, no stranger to late meals,
Galilee host, nodding to Andrew,
'Do what He says!'; picnic begins,
all are filled up and satisfied.

7.

Lady, upper room vigil complete,
overjoyed at Christ's return
from Hades' house of the dead,
help us to break bread once again.

[15 May, 2023]

NEWER POEMS

NINGALOO
The Crisafulli Family, W. A.

Playground, backyard and liquid home
of the humpback whale, gentle dugong,
the manta ray and numerous other species,
the Ningaloo reef is the last bastion, refuge,
corral, borderless sanctuary for sea life.

Wonders of the deep, whaler sharks
with their distinctive reverse polka
dot livery on show. Birds of the air,
from Siberia making for the inland
lake in the desert fed by the ocean.

My sister taking holidays at Ningaloo
with her husband and sons off the reef
living on the beach, grilling the squid,
spangled emperor for lunch and tea
on a barbie, at the edge of the sand.

Author Tim Winton hosts TV show
of this stretch of living coastline,

all his passion for these creatures
brought to bear against big business,
global miners and giant corporations.

Sharks open wide their jaws allowing
fish entry, clearing them of parasites.
Turtles lay dozens of eggs, insurance
against their predators, the ghost crabs.
In March the reef spawns, seeding itself.

Orcas attack humpback whale and calf.
Despite their greater numbers, no kill
today. Failure of commercial whaling
in 1963; rusting tinned remains lying
empty and forlorn at Norwegian Bay.

I once touched a wild creature here,
dolphin vulnerable in the shallows.
What communion was taking place
'twixt the human and the creature?
O N i n g a l o o, O N y i n g g u l u.

[5 June, 2023]

GABY UND HORST

Was für ein grosser Abenteuer, Ihr seid
fünfzig Jahre verheiratet mit Segnen
Gottes. Die Reise mit Schwierigkeiten
begonnen, Horst war schon geheiratet.
Hubert war der treue bayrischer Vater,
der sollte keinen Protestanten seine
Tochter geben. Aber trotz allen dagegen
waren Gaby und Horst am 3 Juli 1973
verheiratet. Sie wohnten am weissen Stein,
und gehen zur Josephskirche in Ginnheim.
Der Tobias betete für die zwei dem Herrn,
"*Gewähre, dass sie und ich Barmherzigkeit
finden können, und dass wir zusammen
alt werden können*"', und sie sagten
beide zusammen: "*Amen, Amen*". [Tobit 8: 8]
So ist es geschehen. Kinder kamen, erstens
Michaela und dann, ein Bub, der Dierk.
Der Horst war kirchentreu und mehr,
Er engagierte sich mit Pfarrgemeinderat.
Ela und Dierk waren ständige Messediener

jeden Sonntag. Dazu kamen die Pfarrfeste und die Feiertage. P. Rohmann hat eine wichtige Entdeckung erfunden. Keine Uberraschung das der Horst katholisch wurde. Domino Gratias!

[8 Juni, 2023]

TIGER TIGER
To Peter Thomas

Cate Blanchett as a tiger, I'd like to see that.
This is a carefully crafted video production,
a full-blooded assault on capitalist markets,
a film shown in the Melbourne Town Hall.

My ticket is a timed entry. I find a seat
to sit down for the session runs for two
hours. The producer is German maestro,
Julian Rosefeldt; me adjusted to the dark,

Brooklyn Youth Choir forms four sides.
to the left and to right, four drum kits
with their drummers flank the action
rearing up on a massive video screen.

Teams: Kyiv, New York, Germany & Sofia.
The sequences follow each other, the taxi
driver and his fare, the arguing vagrants,
assembly line women, the madcap bank

scene, the youth gang, and skater ends up
in a supermart, empty save for the prowler;
cannot recognise Cate, nor her feline voice.
Quotes aplenty, a surfeit of excess & waste.

Drone shots abound, afire New York glitters
at night. *Carmina Burana*, but no Carl Orff,
instead, Blake's tiger stalks the empty aisles
in a crescendo of sound and fury signifying

nothing. Kurt Weill's ballads made Brecht
seeable and doable, we had to wait a bit for
this one, but wait we did. Was it worthwhile?
You the plaintiff, judge, jury and executioner.

Oz society is frightened by the knife gangs,
in our midst, daily stabbings by our youth,
as the USA wrestles with its gun culture,
we battle with those who trust in knives.

Thomas Piketty, on the wealth distribution
in society, is the way forward, but who makes
the first move? The *Waste Land* is alive & well,
and so is the potent tiger prowling among us.

Perhaps the enterprise owes most to Orwell, his fable, *Animal Farm*, the funny and witty parable of the farm animals turning on their masters in a savage satire of our politicians.

[12 June, 2023]

THE NEW BOY
M. S. C. Sisters

Sister and boy meet each other,
adult and child, white and brown,
northern and southern hemisphere
clash in monastic town New Norcia.

Ancient world meets the new age,
but which is old and which is new?
Surprise, things are not as they seem,
Warwick Thornton starts into unknown

country, takes us on a trip where all
is to be found, tasted & experienced.
Five stars out of five? Yes, all of those
And more, in the ratings critics dole

out to endorse their choice selections
bedazzling our timid, tentative views
and our rudderless, double thinking
Mr Orwell has long since canonized.

Sr Cate Blanchett and the new boy,
high stakes, before safeguarding was
was found, three generations later
with its blinding clear denouement.

The child has amazing healing power;
bleeding hands, stigmata, spellbound
by the life - sized Christ in dark wood
mounted up in the community chapel.

The wild boy re-appears, unruly hair
hair neatly combed, the naked torso
demurely clothed in a mission shirt,
baptised, obedient and submissive.

[16 July, 2023]

CHILD OF HILDEGARD

I am a child of Hildegard;
yes, St Hildegard of Bingen
was her baptismal patron saint,
the medieval abbess, polymath,
poet, musician, artist, and ruler
of the Rhineland domain of vines
and fields under the Benedictine
yoke of *ora et labora*, while
the Rhine flowed majestically
below, a mystic, pure and simple.
My mother was teacher, singer,
writer, secretary, knitter, baker
of cakes for parish school fetes
and much later of a poetic circle
to appreciate German literature.

[19 July, 2023]

ORIGINS

'The heavens are telling the glory of God'.
So begins The Creation of Joseph Haydn,
building on the songline created aeons ago
by our Mungo ancestors in the dream-time.

Now a work has been composed by Nicholas
Buc to present us a true harmonious account
how everything came to be following double
helix of Crick & Watson, finders of DNA duo.

Haydn has stood the test of time, will this
fresh oratorio, *'Origins of the Universe,*
of Life, of Species, of Humanity', share
the same praise or join a retinue of failed

operas? It will be interesting to find out.
God doesn't get a guernsey, but Darwin
does, as he is heckled by the unbelievers
as he sings the brand new song Evolution.

Heat has come big time, world is boiling
says UN chief Guterres. Extinctions are
normal, as the environment collapses,
& species begin to vanish from Earth.

Heidelberg Chorale, conducted by Peter
Bandy at the Melbourne Recital Centre.
Today Martha and Mary sit at table with
their raised up brother in Passover meal.

[29 July, 2023]

THE CHESS GAME

As I came up the steps of the Public Library building up to the landing, tense chess game was in progress. I quickly scanned the silent scene and concluded it might be a close match between two equal opponents. Black on attack, White defending, pieces being exchanged and the battle plan simplified. I take a seat despite myself and watch the moves. 4.50 trolleyman appears to collect the remaining chess pieces. Asian contestants shake hands. Crowd departs.

[29 July, 2023]

STRUGGLING WITH ARTIFICIAL INTELLIGENCE

I have difficulties with artificial intelligence; passwords, log-ins, all designed to help you, make you feel incompetent, inferior, sending you back to the classroom. Once I never had a problem, now every session or transaction a contest between me and the computer, AI, as I prefer to call it. Renewing your club dues of membership for the new year fierce contest in four 'simple' steps, purchaser info, member, payment and confirmation. But things go awry, re-setting passwords takes time, if you hang in, things might turn out, if not, you are in a heap of trouble. It's the constant effort of having to prove yourself, wearing you down, leaving you second-rate, non-entity with identity problem When all clicks, you're thinkin' you're dreamin'.

[4 August, 2023]

OPPENHEIMER

Born of German immigrants in the USA
Robert Oppenheimer was asked to head
the *Manhattan Project* to make an atom
bomb before the Nazis had this weapon.

From non-observant Jewish parents he
was fascinated by Hinduism, and above
all, the Bhagavad Gita, & T. S. Eliot's the
Waste Land & Da, Datta and Damyatta.

Earlier at Princeton University he had met
Albert Einstein and asked him about chain
reactions in splitting the atom which might
lead to unstoppable ending of the universe.

With Max Born at Gottingen wrote a thesis.
He researched positrons, dark matter & holes
and assembled the best 50 minds in physics
at the dry *Los Alamos* mesa in New Mexico,

among them Edward Teller, later father of the Hydrogen Bomb, and the English spy, Klaus Fuchs, who betrayed the data to the Russian secret service handlers.

He made a deadly enemy in the Jewish politician Strauss who resented his quirks, arty bohemian life-style, suicidal mistress, left-wing writers and Communist friends.

'If the radiance of a thousand suns were to burst at once into the sky, that would be like the splendour of the mighty one ... I am become Death, shatterer of worlds'.[26]

Trinity was born, later came *Little Boy* and *Fat Man*, dropped by plane on Japan. Oppenheimer visited Truman, stating he *'had blood on his hands'*. The President

snarled: *'I don't want to see that son-of-a-bitch in this office ever again.'* That was not completely true, as fate was to step in

---

[26] Bhagavad Gita, xi, 12

with a Senator from Massachusetts, one

John F. Kennedy voted against Strauss in '59
a top position in Commerce; as President gave
Oppenheimer the Congressional medal in '63;
to make good his rehabilitation as a key public

figure. Oppy was a chain smoker all his life,
succumbing to throat cancer, despite best
treatment, dying in 1967, leaving behind
son, daughter & a deeply grieving widow.

[6 August, 2023]

THE VOICE OF GOD

Mary virgin listened to the voice of God,
brought the Word of God into the world,
may we answer your gentle call and bring
your Son to men and women in our time.

For her mission is not ended continuing
down the ages through generations over
all the earth, alps, falls, steppes, mesas,
plains, lakes, rivers, estuaries & islands.

In hamlets, villages, towns and cities,
the calling occurs, in huts, yurts, flats,
houses & apartments, where the small
still sound of the spirit has been heard.

What do we make of this great discovery?
It comes to us unbidden, yet is heritage
even if not welcomed, invited, accepted
within our inmost shrines and temples.

Birthright like this is inviolable, sacred
as nothing else; but who stands up for
this cause? Who goes in to bat, or puts
up their dukes? Only the crazy, or poets?

We squander, like the prodigal, our gifts,
our inheritance like profligates we are
destined to become, leaving paradise for
a mess of scrambled & scrappy pottage.

Spoken to in a kirk, mosque, synagogue,
stupa, or in the liberating free breath of
the great outdoors of nature, the divine
transcends human categories of thought.

[19 August, 2023]

THE MATILDAS
To Peter Dhuy Thinh Tong

Thank you, Matildas, for a great ride,
right through to the semi-final gainst
the old enemy, England. You played far
above yourselves, demolishing Denmark

first, then going on to win against the
previous world champions, Canadians,
four goals to nil; then came Les Bleus,
the mighty French, in epic penalties,

then it was 1-1 against the Lionnesses
when Sam Kerr scored a goal and the
stadium erupted; alas the English won
three to one; again the Swedes prevailed

by two goals for third place. But Spain
in red turned the feared felines into cats
as they won the trophy, the golden ball
but not the golden glove. Thank you Sam,

Mary, Caitlin, Haley, Alanna, Emily,
Stephanie, Ellie, Kyra, Clare, Katrina,
Charlotte, Cortnee, keeper Mackenzie,
& the others & coach Tony Gustavsson.

The Australian Government has given
200 million dollars to women's sport,
thanks to the Matildas & the exposure
you have won for women everywhere.

[21 August, 2023]

ETHICS OF THE SUMMIT
To Marion Adeney-Steel

You open the newspapers or browse the web and you come across, *"Climbers pass dying man en route to summit."* Shame on all who act like this. It might be a once in a life-time chance to reach an elusive and remote peak, especially in the Himalayas, an intricate big eight thousander; but what is one human life worth? We must do better than this. Putting someone in charge on the mountain to make executive decisions is the least that must be done. Let us start with the Kings: Everest, K2, Kanchenjunga, Lohtse, Makalu, Annapurna I, Cho Oyu, Dhaulagiri I, Manaslu, Nanga Parbat, Gasherbrum I & II, Broad Pk & Shishapangma. These attract climbers from all over the world. They are serviced by professionals who hire sherpas and porters. This has led to laissez faire capitalism and some appalling deaths in the obsessive desire to reach the summit. What about the Queens, seven thousanders,

Gyachung Kang, Annapurna II, Ngadi and
Himal Chuli, Dhaulagiri II, III, IV, V, VI, VII,
Mamostong, Jannu, Makalu II, Nuptse, Fang,
Roc Noir, Jongsang Peak, Gangapurna, Kabru,
Pyramid, Api, Tent Peak, Talung, Chamlang,
Langtang, Baruntse, Pumori, Gauri Shankar,
Nepal Peak, Menlungste, Ganesh Himal I, II,
III and IV; these peaks soar up into the sky,
between heaven and earth, and hang there,
daring the mortals below to approach them
by cliff, crevasse, tower, serac and pinnacle?
Under these are countless others clamouring
for attention, too numerous to mention here.
India, China, Tibet, Nepal & Pakistan host
these mountain spirits among themselves,
& must show some leadership to the West.

[15 September, 2023]

BEETHOVEN'S CHRISTOLOGY[26]
To Anthony Halliday

Beethoven is the master of musical form,
the keys and notes are his to command,
they obey all his wishes and inclinations
perfectly. How do these fit into the grand
narrative that underpins the composition
of the *Hammerklavier* and piano sonatas
110 & 111, then go to the L van B library
in Bonn for the answer, for there is lodged
the thesis of Anthony on the maestro, in
which all is revealed. Here is the perfect
parallel between the Passion of the Christ
in every nuance, exquisitely unfolding in
agonising time and the keyboard mirrors
with shivers of music the awful narration.
By a series of clues, as Handel's Messiah,
on the Death and Resurrection of Christ,
the dedication to the arch-priest Rudolf,

---

[27] The doctoral thesis of Anthony J. Halliday was presented to the Beethoven Museum in Bonn, on 30 July, 2023, under the official title, A resource for performance-interpretation of Beethoven's piano sonatas Opp.106, 110 and 111 in a Christological context. Beethoven Haus, Bonngasse 20, BONN, Deutschland. See Fiona Basile's article in Melbourne Catholics, 29 March, 2023.

Beethoven leads the hearer of the music
from the joy of the repeated Hosannas,
through the dark wood of Gethsemane
to the mocking of Roman legionnaires.
Third movement, 20 minutes in 9 acts,
the longest in all of Beethoven's oeuvre,
Anthony argues, is devoted to the Seven
Words of Christ from the Cross, a genre
created by Hadyn in music, lament and
prayer, climaxing in the phrase, *Pater, in
manus tuas commendo spiritum meum,
Father, into your hands I commend my spirit.*
The fourth movement is set on the Road
to Emmaus, the broken disciples meet
the risen Lord in the breaking of bread.
Instead of finding nothing new, Anthony
has started a whole new world of studies
in the most popular composer of all time.

[31 August, 2023]

ANDAMAN – NICOBAR MISSION
To Jegaraj Hari SSS

The Andaman Mission was accepted 7 years ago by our Indian provincial from Most Rev Bishop Dias' invitation. Three of our religious accepted the call & flew to the isles in the Bay of Bengal hundreds of kilometres from the coast. They were to minister to tribal people, naked as the day that God made them, choosing Port Blair with much easier access, avoiding the convoy system, to control journey through reserves, nor violating the travel ban re tribals segued to the pentecostal missioner from the USA killed five years ago. The Nicobars are over 20% Catholic, live simply, offering food, rice, veg, fruit in lieu of money to the Church. Forbidden by the government to have any contact with them, how could they convert them? Forget the safeguarding

norms and regulations, this is catch 22,
but there is no Viet Nam battleground.

[14 September, 2023]

SIGNS OF LIFE
To John Buckeridge

Planet K2-18b is 8.5 times the size of our home the Earth, a long way, larger than the gas planet Neptune 20 million light years distant away, but it has got the boffins excited out of their minds because it is a water world even having DMS, di-methyl sulphide, vital for life. How do we know all this? Once again thanks to ever reliable JWST, the James Webb Space Telescope, harbinger of info from places beyond our human ken. All this comes from the Professor of Astrophysics at Cambridge Uni.[28] Naturally we are salivating for more, but as the lap dog found out, dry bones do not a juicy dinner make.

[14 September, 2023]

---

[28] The Australian, 'Signs of Life on distant Planet', 14 September 2023, p. 9

THE DATE PALM
To Gerry Kearney SGS

Planted by a dreamer who believed
in the seed that would take time to
grow to fruition, watering, fertilising
the date palm that would some time
in the future not of its choosing,
one day bear fruit in abundance.
The planter did not know the result
of his work which would take eighty
years and he would long be dead.
But the date palm flourished, grew
tall and strong, green and sturdy,
ever reaching to heaven til the
day, the budding fruit was ripe.
Only in one place did it grow,
outside Alice Springs on the
edge of the Simpson Desert.
We had an enchanting morning
tea; fresh date scones offered us
there by the mother of our guide,
en route to Itirkawara (Chambers
Pillar) and his wife (Castle Rock).

[20 September, 2023]

ANNUAL RETREAT 2023

This was a place of great natural beauty set on eastern flanks of Mt Dandenong with lush green lawns, ducks & rabbits, exotic Japanese maples, Norwegian oak, mottled holly, rhododendrons, azaleas, and the cathedral like mountain ash. One kookaburra perched aloft, white cockatoos abounded, magpies chortled We had our rifts and differences. These fissures were not probed, but remained closed. Our retreat director tried hard to open us, but silence was the answer to her invitations. The second last day there was a thaw, symbolic sharing of personal flora. Mine was *lime magic, acacia cognata*, budding leafy fronds screening the deep blue pool marking my baptism into the mystery of Christ.

[28 September, 2023]

CLIMATE CRISIS
To Rhys Arvidson

We are in trouble with the climate,
something our stupidity has made,
releasing huge amounts of methane
and carbon dioxide gas into the air.
Pope Francis warns us that we need
to reduce these now by two degrees.
The alarming news is that we are on
course to exceed this figure, meaning
we are on the threshold point of no
return. A darkened world appears
in deep space, our common home,
Planet Earth, observed by two beings
looking like Michael Leunig's angels [29].

[19 October, 2023]

---

[29] The author wrote an article on the topic of 'Living without fossil fuels', which included a cartoon by Michael Leunig, in November 2023 in the Blessed Sacrament Congregation Newsletter, http://www.stfrancismelbourne.com/doc/one.pdf

HERE C0MES THE SUN
To Melissa Jaffer

Melissa arrived punctually in
Angel driven taxi.[30] I heaved a
sigh of relief when she rang.
I had tried several times to
get her to commit to a talk,
her vocation in the world,
but one way or another, it
had not worked out, falls,
and all seemed lost. Her
teen years, when not in
cold convent at Ballarat,
were at her father's Busy
Bee Hotel, and the rough
side of life, only few doors
from the hallowed church
of St Francis nourishing
the faith of her two sisters,
brother and parents. Seeing
Laurence Olivier in Hamlet

---

[30] Angel was the first name of the taxi driver.

was enough for her to set
her heart on acting as the
preferred profession of life.
Fr Garail pointed to the sun
shine where she would see
God was hidden in all
the scripts eager for her.[31]

[8 November, 2023]

---

[31] Fr Garail was commissioned with executive powers and appointed canonical visitor by the Generalate of the Servants of the Blessed Sacrament Congregation.

SMACKY MAXY

Maxy smacks Cup double ton in Mumbai two weeks after his fastest century. He was cramping up and far from well, all the more amazing feat by an Australian or any other ODI cricketer, saving his country from defeat at 7/91 to victory at 7/293 by Afghanistan batting partner Captain Cummins testifies. He could not walk or run, gave us twenty one fours and ten sixes in his tally. All hail the great Glenn Maxwell, master blaster!

[9 November, 2023]

HEARING CONFESSIONS

Who likes admitting being unable
to hear, to being deaf in fact? No
one, it seems. I have now joined
ranks with no less a maestro
than Ludwig van Beethoven
who first noticed he was going
deaf when he was thirty. All we
have in common is our German
ancestry, but unlike Beethoven
was spared until nearly eighty,
a diminishment of old age, than
a disability of a malfunctioning
faculty. Beethoven was virtually
deaf aged 42. Hearing confessions
becomes onerous and laborious,
a trial and an ordeal, to be endured.
Shyness, reticence and low, soft
voices of penitents make hearing
of confessions arduous and hard.
Greg Manly said penitents came
to make peace with their God, not

with you, the intermediary link.
Jesus, you took pity on those who
were lepers, lame, dumb and deaf;
have compassion and mercy on me.
'*Guard our hearts & tongues from strife;*
From anger's din would hide our life;
From all ill sights would turn our eyes;
Would close our ears from vanities.'[32]

[28 November, 2023]

---

[32] Morning Prayer Hymn, *The Divine Office*, Wednesday, Week Two.

THE NEW GENERAL

We have a new general! He is an Indian!
In the past it was usually a Frenchman,
or at least a French speaker, but now new
ground has been broken, not a European
even, not someone from the New World.
But a new mission region, scarcely 18
years old, which is a teenager Province.
Very Reverend Father Benzy Romician,
General Consultor, Treasurer General,
Local Treasurer of the General House,
Asian Conference, accompaniment of the
Provinces: Kristu Jyoti, Christ the Bread
of Life and Our Lady of the Assumption,
Finance Commission.[33] We wish him well.

[28 November, 2023]

---

[33] https://www.ssscongregatio.org/en/sss-curia/general-consultors.html

SNOOPY, BART AND BLUEY
To All Young of Heart

The Fifties had Charles M. Schulz's cartoon strip Peanuts to delight and amaze tiny toddlers and the young of heart with Woodstock, Snoopy, Charlie Brown, Linus and Lucy; The Nineties had Mat Groening's *The Simpsons*, with Bart, Homer, Marge, Lisa, Mat Flanders and a cast of others. We '*Down Under*' have our beloved and faithful *Bluey*, the blue heeler who has taken the world by the ankles. Not without a scrap, did we have Aussie accents doing the voices of the home grown show that has gone right round the globe, thanks to Queenslander Joe Brumm, who created the family show for his two daughters and oldies, sold it to the BBC Studios and Disney, winning an Emmy on the world stage for children's television.

[17 December, 2023]

SEMINARIANS' DAY IN THE SIXTIES
To John Zika

Seminarians' Day was a gala celebration,
a pause in the daily scholastic horarium.
All the colleges stop their own programs
and everyone comes together to assemble,
fete the new ordinands on their final leg
before they take up their first placements
in the new world that now awaits them all.
The focus soon became the football match,
'Diocesans', the best from Glen Waverley &
Werribee and the 'Religious', from about 12
separate colleges all over metro Melbourne.
It was a slaughter. The religious scratched
their heads and asked, surely we're not that
bad, all we need is some coaching. And so it
was. Tom Hafey was approached, the then
premiership coach at Tigerland. He said
yes, but had an appointment on the day.
No matter, Tommy's Tyroes def. the more
fancied Diocesans and rucks, led by one
George Pell. John Zika remembers playing

for the religious. 'We had a rover who was so fast, from the Jesuits, I think'. Might be Chris Gleason, my researcher informed me.

[24 December, 2023]

THE WORLD SAVED BY BEAUTY[34]
For Kate Hennessy

Long ago I met your grandmother
in Sydney, at Harbord presbytery.
We shared a love of the Russian
novelist Fyodor Dostoyevsky, who
wrote much more than descriptions
of life, but captured the soul of the
people who lived in the time of the
Tzar. The sufferings and struggles
of these sad unfortunate wretches
struck a chord in our spirit, chief
of them, Raskolnikov, redeemed
by the love of the prostitute Sofya,
who gave her life for his in the 1866
novel, Crime and Punishment. We
live in a penal land with our God no
more, for Christ has raised us from
our fallen nature by dying on the
cross in our stead, and we blink
in the strong sunlight of freedom,
amazed at unexpected deliverance.

[10 November, 2023]

---

[34] The phrase, '*The world will be saved by beauty*' is a much loved quotation taken by Dorothy Day from the Fyodor Dostoyevsky novel, '*The Idiot*', where it is used by the protagonist Prince Mishkyn. Kate Hennessy has named her memoir with this title.

www.ingramcontent.com/pod-product-compliance
Lightning Source LLC
Chambersburg PA
CBHW050833010526
44110CB00054BA/2661